EAGLE MEDIA CENTER

DONATED IN HONOR OF
DIANA KATZ
FOR HER SERVICE TO
EAGLE SCHOOL
MAY 1992

CATCH
THAT
CAT!

For Gabriel

CATCH THAT CAT!

A Picture Book of
Rhymes and Puzzles

MONIKA BEISNER

Farrar, Straus and Giroux
New York

I

'Twas in the month of London,
 In the city of July,
The snow was purring softly
 And cats fell from the sky.

A naked girl with clothes on
 Sat standing on a chair.
Three hidden cats were visible,
 But the fourth cat was – where?

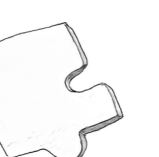

From the dark bush a hellish hound
Appeared to thrust his snout,

But when I took a second look
A harmless cat stepped out.

2

The glutton in the shrubbery
Was enjoying a tasty dish,

When — whoops-a-daisy! he became
A picnic for a fish.

3

4

What a difficult life for a cat!
Shall I do this or do that?
Guzzle my tuna? Lap up my milk?
Or simply flop down on my cushion of silk?
Time for a good caterwaul?
Or to play with my new catnip ball?
A stroll through the garden, then over the fence?
Or would a quick tour of the roof make more sense?
Do whiskers need grooming? Or paws?
I might enjoy sharpening my claws . . .

Oh, yes! It's a difficult life for a cat
With so many choices between this and that.
Right now . . .
                    But I'll leave *you* to tell:
Just arrange these six boxes and see what they spell.

My first is in *chicken*, but not in *hen*.
My second is in *ink*, but not in *pen*.
My third is in *puppet* and also in *toy*.
My fourth is in *monster*, but not in *boy*.
My fifth is in *teddy* and also in *bear*.
My last is in *sunshine*, but not in *air*.
My whole is soft and small and sleek
And likes to hide for you to seek.
Now, riddle my riddle, how many of me
In this cluttered bedroom do you see?

5

Eeny, meeny, midnight mouse
Thinks no one else is in the house:
Out of sight is out of mind,
But how many cat's eyes can *you* find?

Follow the strands
   And spell out the names
Of three fine cats
   Who love playing games.

Five vain cats sitting in a row
Ask the mirror what they want to know:

"Mirror, mirror, on the wall,
Who is the furriest one of all?"

"Mirror, mirror, answer me,
Who has the noblest pedigree?"

"Mirror, mirror, tell me true,
Whose eyes are the bluest blue?"

"Mirror, mirror, speak loud and clear,
Who has the loveliest whiskers here?"

"Mirror, mirror, tell no lies,
Who will win the Cat Show prize?"

But the mirror's only answer, on reflection,
Is a strange and mischievous imperfection . . .

Can you find it?

Listen to me,
    My name is Tom Grey
        And this is my song:
            One fine day
Up in the mountains
    Lying in the grass
        I saw a pussycat
            Sitting on her –
Ask no questions,
    Be not dumb,
        I saw a pussycat
            Sitting on her –
Bumblebees are pretty,
    Bumblebees are kind,
        I saw a pussycat
            Sitting on her –
Behind the mountains
    In the town of Wottom
        I saw a pussycat
            Sitting on her –
Bottomless the ocean,
    Endless the sky . . .
        Now how many pussycats
            Can *you* spy?

Flip and Flop and Flap,
Three garden guardian cats,
Are guarding the cat garden
From rats and bats and brats.
Now tell me, when Flip's eye is on the left of Flop's eye,
And Flap's eye is on the right of Flop's eye,
Is Flip's eye closer to Flop's eye than Flap's eye is,
Or is Flap's eye closer than Flip's eye?

10

Apple trees are many,
    But Cat-trees are few,
So if you find a Cat-tree
    This is what you do:
Look up into its branches
    And with a steady eye
Count all the cats you see there,
    Before you hurry by.

11

1

2   3

4   5

12

Whose shadow is this, can you tell me that?

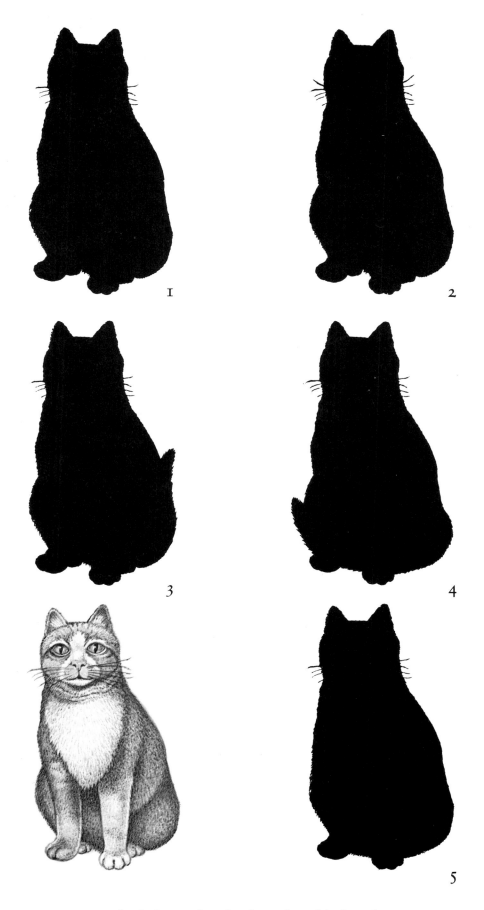

1

2

3

4

5

Now find the right shadow for this lonely cat.

When the sky is velvet and the moon is chalk,
Miranda gets up for her long sleepwalk.

With a cat on her finger and a cat in her hair,
She drifts like a dream through the cold night air.

Her three little kittens disapprove of the sight:
She should be in bed now and tucked up tight.

But she's put on her special embroidered dress,
With a magical meaning that you can guess

If you count the cats on it: their number will tell
The hour she falls under her sleepwalk spell.

13

14

It was a splendid picnic:
    My cat ate two bananas,
My sister chewed some earthworms
    That were sweeter than sultanas,
My rabbit nibbled chocolate cake
    With fruit and ice-cream topping,
My dog devoured a lettuce
    Leaf by leaf, without once stopping,
My cockerel wolfed a sausage,
    And my monkey munched a mouse –
But wait, that doesn't sound quite right.
    Then let's be serious
And work out from the picture
    Whose favorite food was what.
(And as for the things I've told you here,
    You'd best forget the lot.)

Twenty-three kittens all running about;

Two are twins and identical – can you pick them out?

Are these two pictures exactly the same?